THE ULTIMATE TEACHER *Appreciation* GIFT BOOK

THE ULTIMATE TEACHER Appreciation GIFT BOOK

Create, Color, and Fill In a Year of Classroom Memories with the Best Teacher Ever

Illustrated by Annie Brock

Published in the United States by:
ULYSSES PRESS
P. O. Box 3440
Berkeley, CA 94703
www.ulyssespress.com

ISBN: 978-1-64604-026-1
Library of Congress Control Number: 2019951431

Printed in Canada by Marquis Book Printing
10 9 8 7 6 5 4 3 2 1

Managing editor: Claire Chun
Proofreader: Renee Rutledge
Cover design: Jake Flaherty
Cover illustrations: Annie Brock
Interior design and layout: Montague Monsters
Interior illustrations: shutterstock.com: © Gazoukoo; © Es sarawuth; © Bimbim; © balabolka; © edel; © josep perianes jorba; © rangsan paidaen; © Natalia Sheinkin; © peace_art; © Patty Chan

This book is for:

____

From: ____________________

Grade: ____________________

Class of: ____________________

School: ____________________

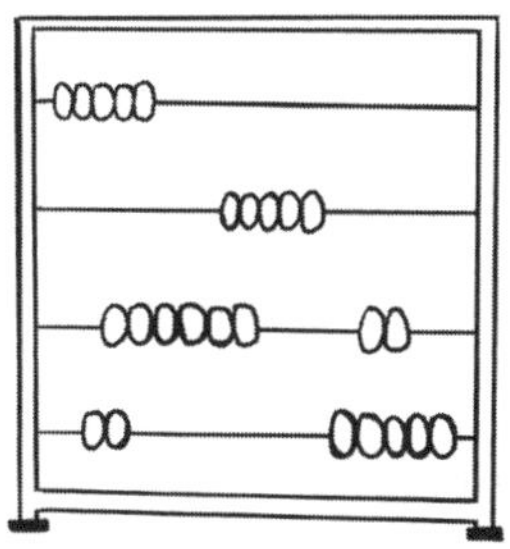

To me, you have been an amazing. . .

T

E

A

C

H

E

R

A picture so you'll always remember me:

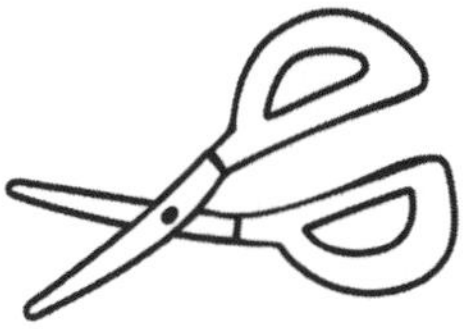  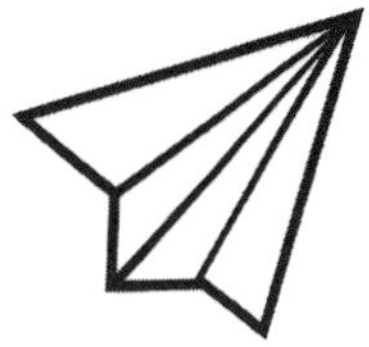

Five things I loved about my class were:

(Outline your hand and write one thing you loved in each finger.)

These are five things I
will remember about you!

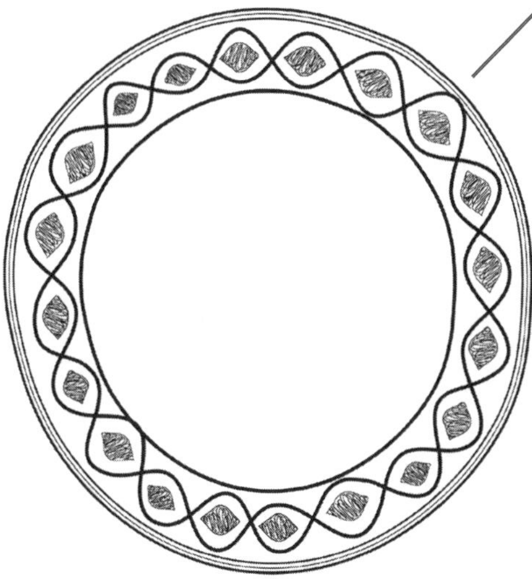

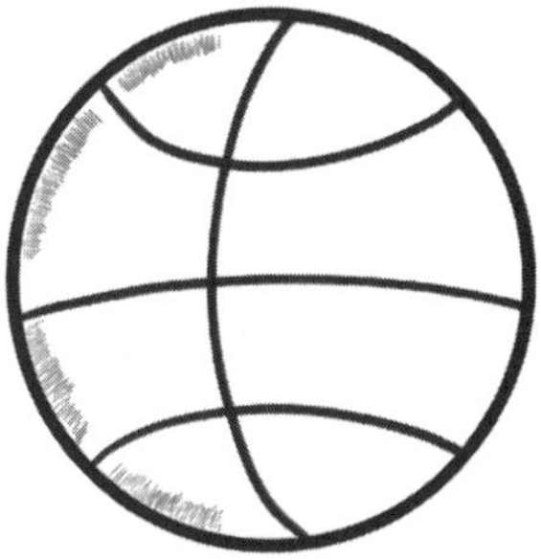

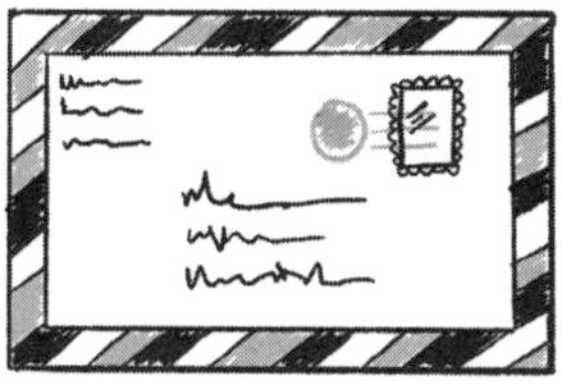

But my favorite memory from this year is definitely:

To me,
the avocation of
a teacher
has something elevating
and exciting.
While surrounded by
the young,
one may always be doing
good.

Dorothea Dix

Coming to class every day made me feel:

I really liked learning about:

The funniest thing you said was:

My favorite part of the day was:

The best field trip we went on was:

But if I could go on any field trip with you, it would be to:

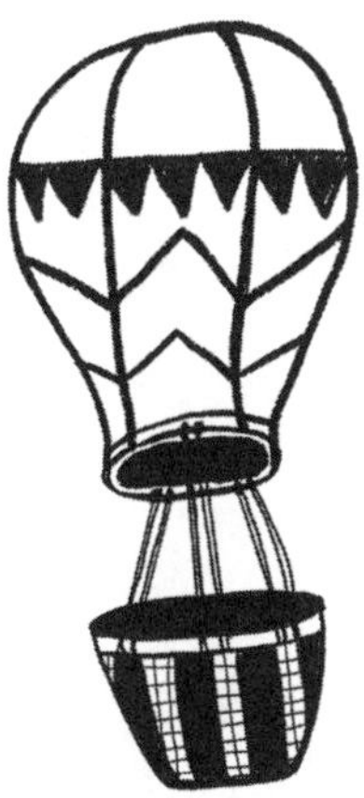

My favorite book we read in class was:

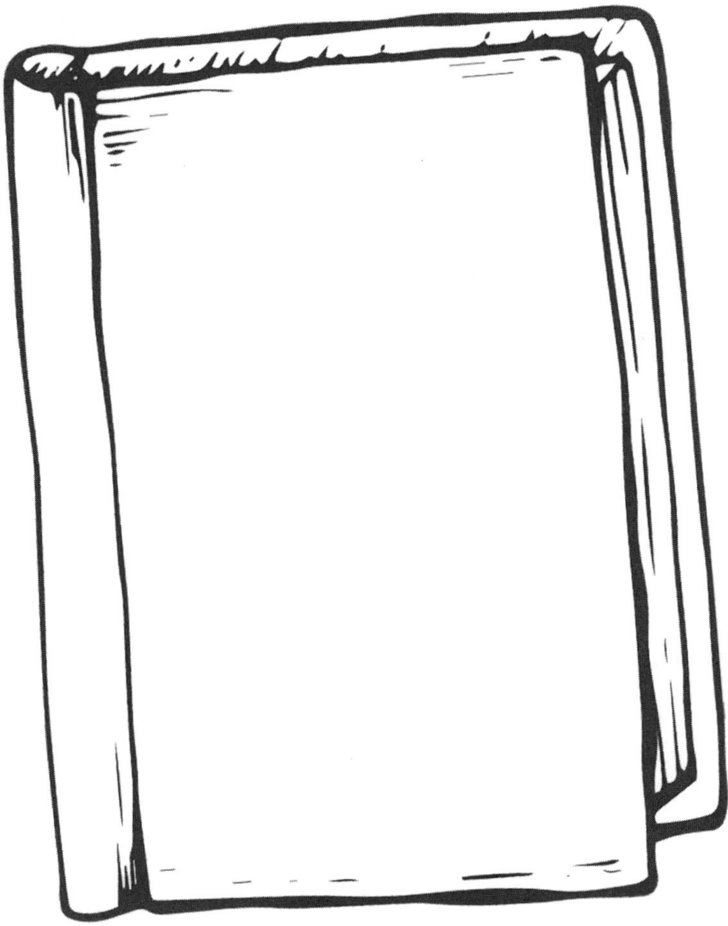

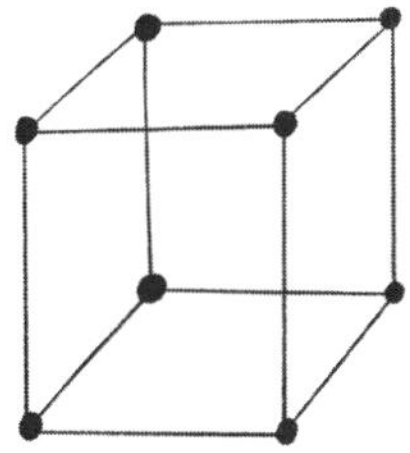

My favorite thing that we learned about this year was:

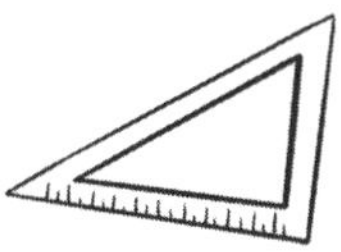
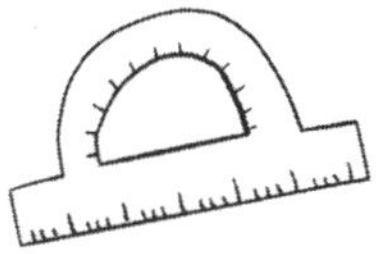
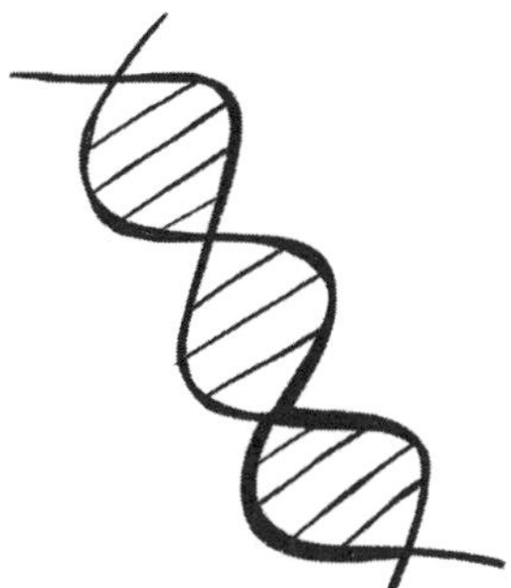

Here is a picture from
one of my favorite days this year:

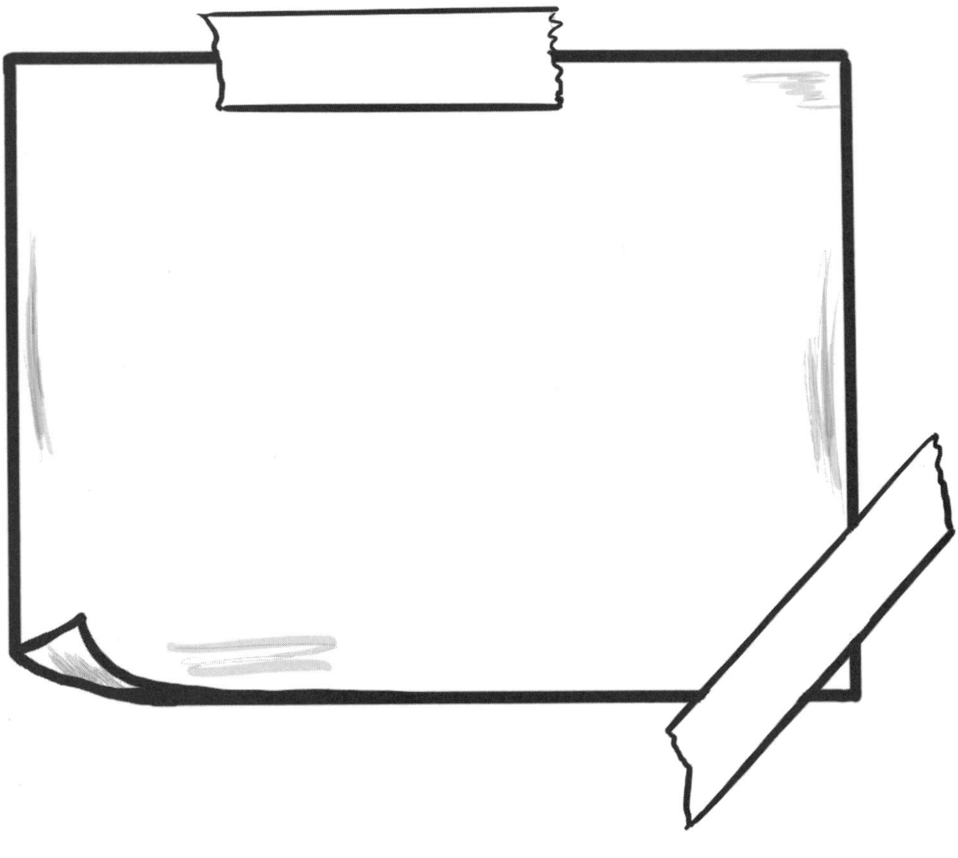

I will miss these three things most about our class:

1 ____

____

2 ____

____

3 ____

____

One child,
one teacher,
one pen,
one book
can change
the world.

—Malala Yousafzai

The best thing about
being your student was:

The best thing about
having you as my teacher was:

You are such a special teacher because:

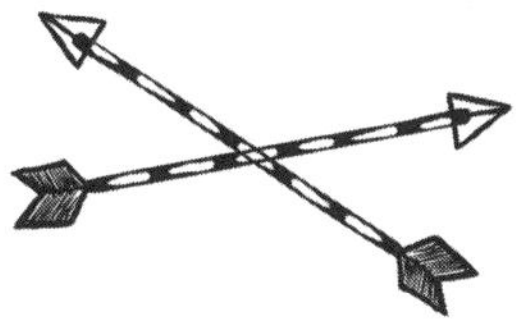

If you were a superhero, you would be:

because. . .

If you were an animal, you would be:

because. . .

If I could get you anything in the world, it would be:

What I'm most excited about for next year is:

I have come to believe that a great teacher

is a great artist

and there are as few as there are

any other great artists.

Teaching might even be

the greatest of the arts

since the medium is

the human mind and spirit.

–John Steinbeck

You deserve a special award

This

Teaching Award

is presented to

....

by ....

A Special Thank You

Dear ______________________________,

Thank You!

____

ABOUT THE ILLUSTRATOR

Annie Brock is a K–12 innovation specialist, and previously taught secondary English and creative writing. She is the coauthor of *The Growth Mindset Coach, The Growth Mindset Playbook, and In Other Words: Phrases for Growth Mindset*. Annie also wrote *Introduction to Google Classroom*. She lives in Holton, Kansas, with her husband, Jared, and their two children. Annie provided the illustrations for *The Growth Mindset Journal*.